WINNING WITH MONEY

the budget tool for people who hate budgets

AARON COLEMAN

russell
media

Boise, Idaho

Published in Boise, Idaho by Russell Media

Web: http://www.russell-media.com

This book may be purchased in bulk for educational, business, or promo-
tional use.

For information please email customerservice@russell-media.com

To learn more about personal finance, the author, or seminars based on the
content contained in this book, please go to http://www.WinningWithMoney.com

ISBN (print):   978-0-9829300-3-8
ISBN (e-book):   978-0-9829300-4-5

Cover design and layout by Drew Steffen.

Printed in the United States of America.

Library of Congress Cataloging-in-Publication Data

Coleman, Aaron Phillip, 1975 ©
    Winning With Money: the budget tool for people who hate budgets / Aaron
Phillip Coleman
        p. cm.
Includes bibliographical references.

ISBN (print):   978-0-9829300-3-8
ISBN (e-book):   978-0-9829300-4-5
1. Self-Help and Personal Finance 2. Business and Personal Finance

Library of Congress Control Number: 2011921807

To my super awesome wife Barb,
who inspires me and so
many others each day.

ENDORSEMENTS

"*Winning With Money* puts the emphasis on the positive. It's not about what you can't buy, it's about having the freedom to know what you can! It's money management without the guilt. Coleman's approach is simple enough to stick with and flexible enough to work for any individual *without* making them feel like a slave to their budgeting system.

GABRIEL M. KRAJICEK
CEO, BancVue Corp.

"*Winning With Money* is a must-read book for anyone wanting to do better at understanding and managing their finances. Aaron Coleman does a great job making a daunting subject simple and practical. His concepts are profound yet accessible to the average person. An extremely relevant book for our culture, *Winning With Money* literally changes the game for personal budgeting and finances. It puts you in control while giving you freedom to make choices and decisions that work for you. Get it today and start winning the money game."

MICHAEL GOGIS
CPA, Chief Financial Officer, Willow Creek Association

"The purpose of budgeting is to create discipline in our financial lives. The key to that discipline is simplicity. Too often, we make maintaining and following a budget so complex that it is doomed to fail from the start. *Winning With Money* offers a simple, easy-to-follow solution to help ANYONE stay within their means. Aaron Coleman's advice on how to think clearly about your financial life will lead to repeatable decisions and behaviors that will get you on your way to *Winning With Money*."

WILLIAM G. GILBERT, JR.
Co-Founder and Partner, The CAPROCK Group, Inc.

"People are capable of anything they put their minds to! With a positive attitude, hard work and a commitment to writing down your goals....you will achieve success. What a gift Aaron has designed for his readers in this well organized, informative and relevant book. I would highly recommend it for anyone wanting to gain control over their finances."

MELANIE SIMBOLI
'88 Olympic Gold Medalist & '89 World Champion, Freestyle Skiing

"The concepts Coleman brings out really hit the nail on the head. Having been involved in finance and financial education my whole career, and having read many books on the subject, this book hits on all the important parts that a person needs to become financially free. I came away wanting to learn and apply again these points that I already knew but needed a reminder. A great book that is so needed in our society."

TODD ERICKSON
CEO, Capital Educators FCU

CONTENTS

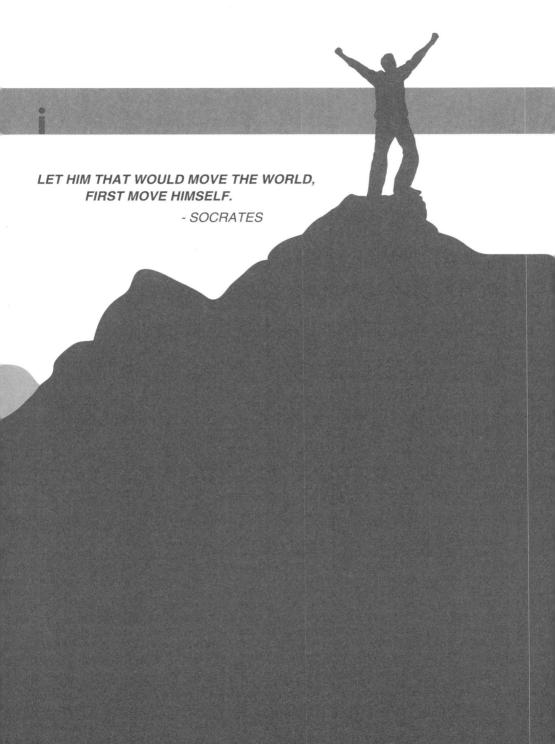

LET HIM THAT WOULD MOVE THE WORLD,
FIRST MOVE HIMSELF.

- SOCRATES

INTRODUCTION

Budgets are far from an exciting topic in to-day's culture. They are not popular. They are not easy. And they certainly are not fun. But let's face it - if you are reading this book – you have some kind of interest in shaping up your finances and getting some control back in your life.

Managing my finances has not always been easy. When I was 22 years old, I was fresh out of college, newly married, with a new job and renting an apartment. We both earned good salaries. It was pretty exciting seeing money in our checking account for the first time. Weird thing happened though – we kept running out of money at the end of each month. We didn't understand. We both had good jobs. We were both responsible people. Why were we running out of money?

> WHY WERE WE RUNNING OUT OF MONEY?

We had heard of budgets before and thought it might be a good idea to try one. The first idea we tried was the "envelope system." That system basically works like this: You figure out how much money you have to spend each month on certain categories – food, clothing, entertainment, gas, household goods, etc… You then go to the bank, pull out enough cash for each of your categories and place that cash into envelopes for each category.

This idea works great for some folks. I respect many of those that endorse this idea. But for my wife and I – this simply did not work. We were both busy individuals with busy lives. Debit cards made sense to us and fit our lifestyle – cash in envelopes did not. As I mentioned, this works for some, just not us. We needed another plan.

We struggled for months, always trying to figure out why we were running out of money. It usually ended up in some sort of fight and blaming each other. Not a good situation under any circumstance – especially for a newly married couple.

We tried the Microsoft Money gig. Certainly a good system, but again, not the right fit for us and the way we lived our lives. I was spending all day on a computer – as was my wife. The last thing we wanted to do when we ended the day was log on to our PC's and see how much money we did not have.

So, I kept thinking. What else can we do? We started to experiment with our own hybrid plan that made sense for us in the way we lived our lives. That plan materialized into the main topic of this book.

This book is about a method and advice to help you manage your cash. I am certainly not a rich man trying to sell you on a "new scheme." I am just like you. I had a problem managing my money – was fortunate enough to develop an idea that has worked for us and a few friends – and thought it just might help others as well.

Why do I think it will help you? It's not a rigid system designed to take away your flexibility and freedom with your spending life. If you want to go out and spend a great night on the town with your spouse – awesome. This book will help you know how much you have to spend on that awesome night out. If you have a really cool pair of shoes you've been looking at for some time, this method will give you the foresight to know when you have enough money to pay for those cool shoes.

This is not a book on complex investing strategies or off-the-wall money management techniques. There are countless thousands of books out there on both of those topics if you are interested. This is simply a book about gaining control of your finances. The main goals in writing this book:

1) This is a book you can finish within a few days. I know many, many people who have started reading books on personal finance to never finish them. This is a book on budgeting – not exactly the most exciting topic. The last thing you need is another boring book to fall asleep to. I encourage you to read this book quickly

and log on to www.WinningWithMoney.
com for support, new ideas and helpful
hints. (And tell your friends about your
new, awesome, budgeting method!)

2) Motivate a positive change of habits. All
good things in life require simple
discipline. Good habits are well-
conditioned disciplines that become a
normal part of a person's life. We often
don't think of good habits and money in the
same sentence – but we should. Simple
money management will help you build
lasting behaviors and ultimately wealth.
And wealth will help generate financial
freedom, flexibility and good stewardship
within your community.

3) Provide a simple tool to help you rest easy
at night. Personal finance keeps so many
within our culture awake at night. The
method we discuss and cover within this
book can help you rest easy – with very
little time commitment. It's so simple; you
don't need a fancy computer or complex
software. If you have a pencil, an eraser
and flat surface – you are on your way!

TAKE THE OFFENSIVE!
The benefit of reading this book is to help you gain a sig-
nificant edge in your life. Life throws at us a number of

obstacles and issues. The better you become at handling these problems - the more fun and fulfillment you experience in life. Conversely, the more frustrated you become, the less control you have over circumstances within your life, creating worry, tiredness and stress.

You work hard for what you earn. Take control of your circumstances and make positive change happen in your life. No one can change your life except for you. It does not happen with gimmicks and hope. It happens when people decide to step up, make a choice to be better, take control and win. Money management – specifically budgeting, is one small step in that process. Budgeting does not have to be a boring, "my parents did that," kind of thing. It should be a motivating exercise that allows you to live a dynamic, more "in control" life than you do today.

MY EXPERIENCE

My sister-in-law came over one day shortly after we started using The *Winning With Money* Method. She saw the budget on the refrigerator, stared at it for a minute, and started laughing, "Are you serious with this?"

Feeling a little embarrassed, "Well, yeah, kind of."

She laughed louder, "Please tell me you put this away when friends come over."

"Oh yeah, I just forgot."

I was so frustrated. I finally found a system that worked for us and a college kid was laughing at me. I started hiding the budget when people came over in order to avoid more humiliation. However, as time went on, The *Winning With Money* Method really worked for us and was helping us meet our financial goals. After a couple of years, I started displaying our budget with confidence. (Not that it showed I had lots of money by any means – I think our first calendar had a whopping $11.00 per day.) Before long, friends began to comment on the strange calendar we had on the side of the fridge. It sparked many conversations. Soon, I found out that many of our friends were struggling with the same financial issues we faced and were desperate for more control.

About seven years after my sister in law first laughed at my budget, she approached me one day. She asked if we were still doing our refrigerator budget. I said we were. She smiled, laughed a little, and finally asked if I could teach her how to do it. Absolute Vindication!

GAME CHANGERS RULE!

Money is hard work. The American education system does a very poor job in teaching our society even the basic principles of personal finance. I could cite multiple statistics on the dire reality of American savings rates, debt loads and bankruptcy filings. But I won't. You know the story.

The numerous books, magazines, newspapers and television shows dedicated to money management intimidate many Americans. "Aren't those just for wealthy people?" "I don't have time for that stuff." "Heck, I don't have enough money anyway."

A company I previously worked for has a saying they applied to a culture shift in their industry: Game Changers Rule! It's time to change your game. The goal behind this book is to end the frustration of running out of money before the next pay period – to end the frustration of having to go into debt to make ends meet. *Winning With Money* is designed to give you some simple tools and simple disciplines to help you better manage your money. You can do it. If you make up your mind that you want more freedom, flexibility and options in your financial life – this book will provide you with a base foundation to achieve that.

IT'S TIME TO CHANGE **YOUR** GAME.

Freedom:
When you are not controlled by money – you have freedom that extends deep into your soul. You are not owned by it. You sleep better, you feel better, and you have more fun in life.

Flexibility:
Having control of your money gives you flexibility. Instead of being forced into a decision, you can choose your path. You have the ability to try different things and make bold decisions you might not otherwise make.

Options:
My good friend Mark Hallahan has always told me, "Save your money – it gives you options." Options are nice to have in life. If you want to

switch jobs, a big bank account makes it a little bit easier. If you want to go on a cool vacation, knowing your financial picture will allow you to determine where and how long. A solid bank account gives you those options.

If you are willing to spend five minutes a day – you can begin to take control of your day-to-day finances without a cumbersome, difficult process of a full-scale budget. I hope you find the The *Winning With Money* Method a fun, fast read and springboard to financial freedom in your life.

If you only take a couple of key points away from this book, a handful of new strategies that will work for you or your family – then this book is a success. If you finish this short book and as a result have more Freedom, Flexibility and Options in your life, then excellent! That's the whole point in reading this book.

IMPORTANT NOTE:

However, if after reading this book you still haven't found a solution – no problem. The fact that you have read this far means you have a genuine interest in cleaning up your personal finances. Come to www.WinningWithMoney.com to research other money management tools and techniques. You will soon be winning with your money.

OK, I'm in. What's in the book?

Winning With Money is really broken into two, easy to read sections. The first section is going to focus on The *Winning With Money* Method for setting up your budget and managing your daily spending money. You will learn why a budget is important, how The *Winning With Money* Method works and how to make it work for you.

Specifically, we will focus on three main areas: Identify, Understand and Execute.

1)   Identify
You first must identify some things in your financial life before you can begin to fix them:
-        What is your income?
-        What are your monthly obligations (bills, payments, etc…)?

2)   Understand
Once you have indentified the key areas in your finances, you need to understand how they all fit together.
-        How much are you spending on bills?
-        How far is your income reaching?
-        What do you have left over at the end of each month?

3)   Execute
Now that you have identified and understand your situation, it's time to make a plan and make it work for your lifestyle. Again, this book is not going to tell you how much you can spend on entertainment, coffee, baseballs, beer or anything else. It is going to provide you with a tool to help you understand how much money you have to work with on a daily basis.

The second half of the book is going to focus on six financial principles that are important to understand. These principles are not complicated or complex. They are things to think about and integrate into your lifestyle as you gain success in your financial life. Included topics:

Chapter 6:   Building your Emergency Fund
                    (or the GTH Fund)
Chapter 7:   Understanding Debt
Chapter 8:   Investments
Chapter 9:   Net Worth: What's that?
Chapter 10: Giving Back
Chapter 11: Setting Goals

At the end of each chapter, there will be two questions for you to think about. Grab a pen or pencil and jot down what comes to mind. This is certainly not mandatory. It's simply a chance to reflect on your own situation and organize your thoughts.

The more energy and thought you put into thinking through your issues, the quicker you begin to solve them.

i

QUESTIONS:

1)   What is the ONE thing you hope to gain by
     reading this book?

2)   How much time do you currently spend managing
     your personal finances each week?

WINNING WITH MONEY

WHY MANAGE YOUR MONEY?

> "Success is not final,
> failure is not fatal:
> it is the courage to continue that counts."
>
> **WINSTON CHURCHILL**

If you want to win with money, you have to manage your money. Most people simply don't take the time to manage their money. That's too bad. Banks, retailers and corporations make A LOT of money because the average American doesn't take the time to truly understand their money and manage their funds wisely.

Let's start by explaining how banks (and credit unions) make money. Banking in all actuality is a very simple business. Banks make money two primary ways: through sound banking practices and their customers' mismanagement of money.

Bankers traditionally make their money by lending and investing. Bankers attract money to their bank by offering a rate of return for those dollars (or deposits). You have all seen advertisements for banks and credit unions offering a CD at 2.5%, a money market account paying 2% or savings account paying 1.5%. By offering these rates, they entice people to deposit their money with their particular bank. This, in general, is a good thing. People need a safe place to keep their money and banks need money to stay in business.

Banks also attract money by offering people a free service in return for their money – i.e. free checking. You as the consumer get the advantage of storing your short-term cash in a safe place with access to checks, ATM's, debit cards, online banking and a teller window.

Once a banker has your money in their bank – they make a return on those dollars by either lending it out – or investing. In the lending sense, the banker lends the money out at various rates. Maybe a car loan at 8%, a home loan at 6% or a business loan at 7%. The difference between the loan rate and the deposit rate is called the "spread." For example:

If a banker brings in money in a savings account at 1.5%, and they lend those dollars out to a small business at 7%, the spread between the two is 5.5%.

Bankers also will take deposit dollars and invest those dollars in the various capital and government markets available to them. A good banker will work very hard to find great investments. Other bankers are not so fortunate. Because many bankers were not as good as others – banks created some new investment options. Without going into too much detail – it is these new investment options that in part led to the 2008 – 2009 financial meltdown.

The second way bankers make money is by charging their customers fees. Banks call this fee income, or non-interest income. Fee income comes in four main forms: 1) Interchange fees, 2) Fees for services, 3) Credit Card fees and 4) Overdraft fees. The consumer does not have much to do with interchange fees (the bank makes money from the merchant every time you swipe your debit and credit card at the store), so let's focus on the three you do have control over.

a.   Banks charge their customers and non-customers specific fees for services. Mortgage service fees and other loan fees make up a large majority of this category. The most personal example of this fee in the marketplace is the fee a bank charges people to use their ATM. If you are the customer of that bank, the ATM is free to use. If you are not a customer of that bank and you use their ATM, you will most likely be charged a fee of $2.00 to $3.00.

Some banks also charge their customers fees for certain checking and savings accounts. Be careful when opening your accounts to make sure you know exactly what you are going to be paying for that account each month. With your personal funds, I highly recommend opening an account that does not charge you a fee just to have the account.

b.   Banks offer these really cool, handy pieces of plastic that many of us have in our wallets. They come in fancy colors, have your name on them, and generally make you feel real good about yourself every time you use them. And guess what, banks make a ton of money on you keeping these things in your wallet. In fact, in 2009, banks made $20.5 billion in credit card penalty fees.

CREDIT CARDS WILL **EAT YOU ALIVE** IF YOU ARE NOT VERY CONSCIOUS AND RESPONSIBLE IN THE WAY THAT YOU USE THEM.

While I am not on the anti-credit card bandwagon that some are on – I will say this: Credit cards will eat you alive if you are not very conscious and responsible in the way that you use them. I have a short chapter in the back of this book dedicated to credit cards, so I won't beat the proverbial dead horse here. Just know this: Credit Card fees are very expensive. If you fail to pay off the balance of your credit card each month, you will be charged an interest charge of up to 30%. If you are late with your payment, you are charged a very stiff penalty. When you start looking at interest charges of 25-30%, that can compound very quickly and cost you a lot of money.

Credit cards are really cool if you have the cash and discipline to pay them off each month. It's like and interest free loan for 30 days. BUT – most people don't pay their cards off each month – or on time, and then guess what happens – you get hit with ginormous fees and the viscous debt cycle begins. You get poorer; the bank gets richer. Not a good scenario unless you're the bank!

c. Overdraft fees are also a big winner for the banks. In 2009, banks in the United States collected $38.5 Billion in overdraft fees. If you have $10 in your account, and you write a check for $15, you overdraw your account for $5. Many people know this practice as "bouncing a check." When this happens, the bank is going to charge you a fee for overdrawing your account. This is usually between $20 and $35 each time you overdraw your account. If you overdraw your account 20 times in a month, that could be up to $700 in fees that come right out of your account. Ouch! It is tough to be *Winning With Money* under that scenario.

Now that you know how banks make money – let's focus in on how to make sure they don't make it with your money!

QUESTIONS:

1) Do you feel you "waste" money each month because you don't have a plan?
2) Did you pay your bank any overdraft fees or credit card fees last year? How much?
3) What are you going to do about it going forward?

IDENTIFY

Winning With Money is all about helping you WIN with your finances. The next couple of chapters are going to explain a simple, yet powerful tool to help you identify a daily amount of discretionary spending you can use or save as you see best for your situation.

Most good businesses start off each year with objectives and goals they want to achieve. They plan how much money they are going to spend, how much they are going to make, and forecast a profit to attain at the end of that year. You as individuals and families need to do the same thing. It does not have to be a complicated process. In fact, it should actually be a fun process. Look at your income each month and how much you spend each month. If you earn more money than you spend, the difference is your profit – to do with whatever you please: save, spend, give, etc…If you spend more money than you earn, then that's a loss or debt.

By having a profit – you gain the freedom, flexibility and options we discussed in the previous chapter. This allows you to truly live as you were intended to live – with passion, vigor and happiness, free from the stressful and often unnecessary burden of personal finance hell.

As I have mentioned, this will not be a complicated process – and it's not. To help us better walk through this process and understand the concepts within this book, I would like to introduce a family that we will follow through the next couple of chapters: Bill and Mary Smith. (Yes, very original and very cool people.)

Bill and Mary are both 35 years old, have been married for seven years and have two young children of three and five. Both Bill and Mary work outside of the home. Bill is a supervisor at a local technology company and Mary is a schoolteacher at a nearby elementary school. They live in the suburbs with little access to public transportation.

The Smith's have worked hard – both excelling at their jobs. They are smart, educated people and committed to making a better life for their family. They currently earn about $75,000 between them, save money each month in their 401K (8%), and each have reasonable health insurance. But like many people in the same position, running out of money at the end of each month frustrates them. They are frustrated with credit card bills. They are discouraged and feel stuck and not quite sure why.

To add to their frustration, Bill and Mary have always wanted to take a big vacation to Europe and hike the Swiss Alps. Every time they try to price the trip, they realize there is no way to pay for it without going into major debt. They go back and forth, attempting to make it happen, but usually give up and quit discussing it.

We will use Bill and Mary's situation to outline where they are at now and help them create a plan to get them on the right footing.

The first step in creating a budget for any family or individual is identifying your current situation. Quite simply, what is your income each month and what bills and other obligations do you have to pay each month.

INCOME

Knowing your income is usually a pretty simple process. Most people know how much money they are going to make each month. If you work varied hours or on a commission structure – do your best to estimate what you make. (If you really fluctuate each month, we'll circle back to that in chapter 5.)

For this method, we are not too concerned with your gross income – what matters is your net income – or take home pay – how much money actually ends up in the bank after deductions and taxes.

In this case, the Smith's combined take home pay is $4,500 per month.

(see Bill and Mary's paychecks on the following pages)

THE FIRST STEP IN CREATING A BUDGET FOR ANY FAMILY OR INDIVIDUAL IS IDENTIFYING YOUR CURRENT SITUATION.

BILL'S PAYCHECK

0068-H795
100 Payroll

DATE	CHECK NO.
09/08/2010	10207

PAY TO THE
ORDER OF

BILL SMITH
1000 ANYROAD
MIDDLE, KANSAS

Total Net Direct Deposit(s)
$2,680.59
AMOUNT

VOID THIS IS NOT A CHECK .... DOLLARS

NON-NEGOTIABLE
AUTHORIZED SIGNATURE(S)

FOLD AND REMOVE

FOLD AND REMOVE

PERSONAL AND CHECK INFORMATION
BILL SMITH
1000 ANYROAD
MIDDLE, KANSAS

Soc Sec #: xxx-xx-8614   Employee ID: 1
Home Department: 100 Payroll

Pay Period: 08/01/10 to 08/31/10
Check Date: 09/08/10   Check #: 10207

NET PAY ALLOCATIONS

EARNINGS	DESCRIPTION	HOURS	RATE	THIS PERIOD ($)	YTD HOURS	YTD ($)
	Regular	GROSS →		3750.00		30000.00
	EARNINGS			3750.00	1386.0	30000.00

WITHHOLDINGS	DESCRIPTION	FILING STATUS	THIS PERIOD ($)	YTD ($)
	Social Security		157.50	1260.00
	Medicare		54.38	434.04
	Fed Income Tax		232.00	1856.00
	KS Income Tax		167.03	1336.24
	TOTAL		610.91	4887.28

DEDUCTIONS	DESCRIPTION	THIS PERIOD ($)	YTD ($)
	401(k)	300.00	2400.00
	Medical	158.50	1268.00
	TOTAL	458.50	3668.00

NET PAY	NET →	THIS PERIOD ($) 2680.59	YTD ($) 21444.72

Payrolls by Paychex, Inc.

2 . **IDENTIFY**

MARY'S PAYCHECK

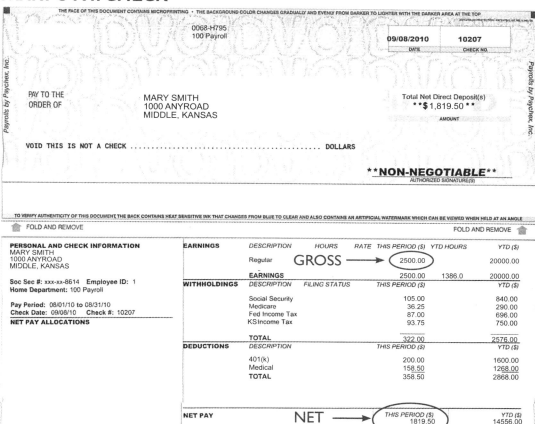

THE FACE OF THIS DOCUMENT CONTAINS MICROPRINTING • THE BACKGROUND COLOR CHANGES GRADUALLY AND EVENLY FROM DARKER TO LIGHTER WITH THE DARKER AREA AT THE TOP

0068-H795
100 Payroll

09/08/2010	10207
DATE	CHECK NO.

PAY TO THE
ORDER OF

MARY SMITH
1000 ANYROAD
MIDDLE, KANSAS

Total Net Direct Deposit(s)
$1,819.50
AMOUNT

VOID THIS IS NOT A CHECK .... DOLLARS

NON-NEGOTIABLE
AUTHORIZED SIGNATURE(S)

TO VERIFY AUTHENTICITY OF THIS DOCUMENT, THE BACK CONTAINS HEAT SENSITIVE INK THAT CHANGES FROM BLUE TO CLEAR AND ALSO CONTAINS AN ARTIFICIAL WATERMARK WHICH CAN BE VIEWED WHEN HELD AT AN ANGLE

FOLD AND REMOVE   FOLD AND REMOVE

PERSONAL AND CHECK INFORMATION
MARY SMITH
1000 ANYROAD
MIDDLE, KANSAS

Soc Sec #: xxx-xx-8614   Employee ID: 1
Home Department: 100 Payroll

Pay Period: 08/01/10 to 08/31/10
Check Date: 09/08/10   Check #: 10207

NET PAY ALLOCATIONS

EARNINGS	DESCRIPTION	HOURS	RATE	THIS PERIOD ($)	YTD HOURS	YTD ($)
	Regular	GROSS ➝		2500.00		20000.00
	EARNINGS			2500.00	1386.0	20000.00

WITHHOLDINGS	DESCRIPTION	FILING STATUS	THIS PERIOD ($)			YTD ($)
	Social Security		105.00			840.00
	Medicare		36.25			290.00
	Fed Income Tax		87.00			696.00
	KS Income Tax		93.75			750.00
	TOTAL		322.00			2576.00

DEDUCTIONS	DESCRIPTION		THIS PERIOD ($)			YTD ($)
	401(k)		200.00			1600.00
	Medical		158.50			1268.00
	TOTAL		358.50			2868.00

NET PAY	NET ➝	THIS PERIOD ($)	YTD ($)
		1819.50	14556.00

Payrolls by Paychex, Inc.

Payrolls by Paychex, Inc.

FIXED COSTS

It is also imperative to know your monthly bills and obligations. I call this your fixed costs. How much are you spending each month on your utilities, cable, day care, subscriptions, etc...? I have included a form to help you indentify these items on page 40 and in the back of the book. (These forms are also available at www.WinningWithMoney.com.) Simply write in the amount you spend each month for each category. If it varies, use an average.

Bill and Mary live a pretty modest lifestyle and have lived by reasonable financial principles most of their lives. Their expenses are in line with where they should be for their current income situation (opposite page):

FIXED COSTS WORKSHEET (blank in back)
The bills you know you always have to pay:

Mortgage	$ 1,100
Rent	$
Student Loans	$ 250
Car Loans	$ 200
Power	$ 100
Gas	$ 20
Water	$ 50
Phones	$ 100
Television	$ 65
Dry cleaning	$
Day care	$ 300
Tithe	$ 50
Neighborhood Dues	$
Other dues/memberships	$
Tuition	$
City	$ 50
Insurance	$ 100
Prescriptions	$ 50
Other	$
Other	$
Other	$
Other	$
Other	$

TOTAL	$2,435

MONTHLY ESSENTIALS

Monthly essentials are items you know you will have to pay for each month – but sometimes vary. Things like food and gasoline. It's a good idea to list these out as well so you have a good understanding of what you will be spending over and above your fixed costs.

The Smith's, similar to many hard working families, like to eat. And with two small children running around, having food in the house is important. Bill drives about 20 miles each day to and from work – Mary, only about 5. So their gas budget is also important. It's tough to get to work if you don't have transportation.

Variable Costs

Food per month	$400
Gasoline per month	$250
Other	$____
TOTAL	**$650**

> YOU MIGHT BE SURPRISED IF YOU HAVE NEVER DONE THIS EXERCISE TO LEARN HOW MUCH YOU SPEND EACH MONTH.

The process of identifying and listing out each of the previous items: Net income, Fixed Costs and Monthly Essentials is the first vital step in creating a budget. It might take a little time to corral all your bills and determine your fixed costs, but it is very worth the time. You might be surprised if you have never done this exercise to learn how much you spend each month. If you do nothing else in this book – go through this step.

2

QUESTIONS:

1)   Are your fixed costs higher than what you
     thought they were?

2)   What cool adventure or purchase have you always
     wanted – but never had the money to accomplish?

All right. Now you are gaining a better grasp of your income and spending. Here comes the fun part – how much can you spend each month? The *Winning With Money* method really starts to play out in this chapter. (All the information contained in this chapter, including the forms you need are located at www.WinningWithMoney.com.)

Bill and Mary completed their first steps; so let's take a look at where they end up.

> **Step 1:** Going back to the last chapter – they have their take home income figure. That is going to be our first step.
>
> > *Identify how much money they take home per month:* about **$4,500**
>
> **Step 2:** Now, we take their fixed costs figure from the last chapter: **$2,435**
>
> **Step 3:** We need to identify what's left over? (Simply subtract Step 2 from Step 1): **$2,065**

Step 4: We also identified the Monthly Essentials in the previous chapter. Now, list those costs out:

Food per month	$400
Gasoline per month	$250
Other	$_____
Other	$_____
TOTAL:	**$650**

Step 5: What's left over? Simply subtract Step 4 from Step 3: **$1,415**
(Notice they are still positive. If this was not the case, we discuss what to do in Chapter 5.)

Step 6: Bill and Mary are also setting aside cash in savings each month. (We will discuss the benefits of having a solid savings account in the second half of this book.) They are saving $300 each month.

Subtract Step 6 from Step 5: **$1,115**

Step 7: Finally! We are at the crux of The Winning With Money Method!!! We now get to determine their daily spending amount. They have identified their income, their bills and their daily essentials. They now have an amount of cash left over that they get to live on. Notice, I did not write, "how much they get to categorize for movies, ice cream, shoes and software…" What you do with your daily amount is completely at your discretion. If you really like ice cream and want to spend $10.00 a day on it – go for it!

We take the amount from Step 6 and divide it by the number of days in their pay period – or month. (Your pay period might be weekly, every two weeks, every month, etc…

Amount from Step 6: $1,115 / 28 (number of days) in pay period = $40.00 per day.

This is Bill and Mary's *Winning With Money* Daily Spend number.

Step 8: Last, we take each of the Monthly Essentials from Step 4 and divide by 4. This will give them an amount that they can spend each week on Food and Gas.

Food per month:
$400 / 4 = $100 per week
Gasoline per month:
$250 / 4 = $62.50 per week

Beginning on the following page is a blank form for you to walk through the same exercise. You can also go to www. WinningWithMoney.com and fill in your information:

WINNING WITH MONEY WORKSHEET

Step 1: Identify how much money you take home per month. (After all withdrawals) $_____

Step 2: Subtract out your fixed costs – or bills you know you always have to pay. Use actuals.

Fixed Costs:

Mortgage	$_____
Rent	$_____
Student Loans	$_____
Car Loans	$_____
Power	$_____
Gas	$_____
Water	$_____
Phone	$_____
Television	$_____
Dry cleaning	$_____
Day care	$_____
Tithe	$_____
Neighborhood Dues	$_____
Other dues/memberships	$_____
Tuition	$_____
City	$_____
Insurance	$_____
Prescriptions	$_____
Other	$_____
Other	$_____
Other	$_____
TOTAL:	$_____

Step 3: What's left over?
(Subtract Step 2 from Step 1): $_____

You now have a bucket of money left over.
How much of that are you going to spend on essentials,
i.e. Food and Gasoline?

Step 4: Essential Costs

Food per month $_____
Gasoline per month $_____

TOTAL: $_____

Step 5: What's left over now?
(Subtract Step 4 from Step 3): $_____

Step 6: How much are you going to save????
      $_____

Step 7: Determine your Daily Spend.
Subtract Step 6 from Step 5: $_____

Divide this amount by the number of days
    In your pay period: $_____

    Daily Spend Total = $_____

Step 8: Monthly Essentials: Take each from Step 4 and divide each by 4.

Gas $_____
Food $_____

- - -

This chapter really is the difference between winning and losing with money. Take the time to pound through these steps and, at the very least, you will better understand where you are spending your money each month.

QUESTIONS:

1) Is your daily figure more or less than you
   thought it would be?

2) Are you currently setting any savings aside
   each month?

EXECUTE

BUILDING YOUR CALENDAR

Getting your *Winning With Money* figure is crucial to setting up your budget. The second part is setting up your monthly calendar. The calendar is completely customized for your situation. It is created each month for you based on your *Winning With Money* figure. In fact, visit www. WinningWithMoney.com; input your simple figures and we will create the calendar for you!

Your calendar is made up of three parts: Daily Spend, Food, and Gas (or other important categories in your life.) The Daily Spend is the main piece of the calendar. This is the amount from Step 6. Just like it sounds, this is the amount you have available to spend each day – if you were to spend the same amount each day. Now we know that is not the case, so we will show you how to manage this number.

Let's look first at the Daily Spend:

Each day on the calendar is broken into three areas:

A = AVAILABLE: How much money you have available to spend that day, YOUR WINNING WITH MONEY amount.

U = USED: How much you actually spent that day.

D = DIFFERENCE: What is the difference between what you had Available and what you actually Used (spent).

$X / day

Sun 4	Mon 5	Tues 6	Wed 7	Thurs 8	Fri 9	Sat 10
A:	A:	A:	A:	A:	A:	A:
U:	U:	U:	U:	U:	U:	U:
D:	D:	D:	D:	D:	D:	D:

We identified Bill and Mary's *Winning With Money* amount as $40.00. For Day 1, we simply put their *Winning With Money* amount next to the "A" on the first day on the calendar.

$40 / day

Sun	4	(+)	5	Tues	6	Wed	7	Thurs	8	Fri	9	Sat	10
A: $40				A:		A:		A:		A:		A:	
U:				U:		U:		U:		U:		U:	
D:	D:			D:		D:		D:		D:		D:	

The calendar above illustrates that they have $40.00 in the
Available column to spend on Sunday the 4th. Bill and Mary
decided to go to the Sunday afternoon matinee and spent
$40.00. So they would write in $40.00 in the Used column.
This would mean at the end of the day, they have a $0.00
balance on their calendar. Example:

$40 / day

Sun	4	Mon	5	Tues	6	Wed	7	Thurs	8	Fri	9	Sat	10
A:	$40	A:		A:		A:		A:		A:		A:	
U:	($40)	U:		U:		U:		U:		U:		U:	
D:	$0	D:		D:		D:		D:		D:		D:	

Now, because they spent the full $40.00 daily allotment,
they do not have any balance to carry over to the next day.
They simply have another $40.00 available to spend for that
next day. Example:

$40 / day (+)

Sun	4	Mon	5	Tues	6	Wed	7	Thurs	8	Fri	9	Sat	10
A:	$40	A:	$40	A:		A:		A:		A:		A:	
U:	($40)	U:		U:		U:		U:		U:		U:	
D:	$0			D:		D:		D:		D:		D:	

Monday is a working day for the Smith's. Bill decides to pack his lunch for the day. He has onsite meetings all day and the company cafeteria is run by an old lady who forgot how to cook in the 80's, so brown bagging it is fine with Bill. Mary on the other hand REALLY likes to stop by the local coffee shop on her way to school for her double shot, non-fat, grande vanilla latte. (And who could blame the lady – she teaches second grade...) But today – she is trying extra hard to stay in budget and decides to forgo the coffee and drink the cheap brand in the teachers' lounge. The coffee is not good, but does the trick. Upon the days end, the Smith's are quite tuckered out. They feed the kids a simple dinner, get them to bed and settle in for a night of reading.

Consequently, they don't spend any money on the 5th. They would enter a $0.00 in the Used row for that day. The Difference row will show $40 ($40 Available minus $0 Used equals $40 Difference). Awesome! Woohoo! They get to roll the Difference into the next day. So on Tuesday, they have a whole $80 in their Available row.

Example:

$40 / day						
Sun 4	Mon 5	Tues 6	Wed 7	Thurs 8	Fri 9	Sat 10
A: $40	A: $40	A: $80	A:	A:	A:	A:
U: ($40)	U: $0		U:	U:	U:	U:
D: $0	D: $40		D:	D:	D:	D:

4 . EXECUTE

The Difference, either **positive** or **negative**, is always rolled over to the next day.

Tuesday is a big day for the Smith's. Bill has a lunch meeting scheduled and needs to buy a new shirt and tie for a meeting he has planned at the end of the week. He ends up spending $85 dollars. They only have $80 budgeted, but it was a needed item. No problem. Mary was willing to forgo her morning ritual and choke down the cheap coffee for another morning, but needed to buy a new pair of shoes for each of the kids. She spent a total of $50 for both kids. Which brings up a good point. Bill and Mary communicated with each other. Bill told Mary what he needed to do and they both agreed that they needed to purchase what they did. They communicated – and that is a critical piece in ANY financial solution you put in place for your situation. We will talk this through further in Chapter 5.

The point is knowing exactly where you stand at all times, so you can manage your money to end each month in the positive.

Since they had $80 to start with and they spent $135, they are now in the hole with a negative $55 balance. (So much for the "awesome and

> THE POINT IS KNOWING EXACTLY WHERE YOU STAND AT ALL TIMES, SO YOU CAN MANAGE YOUR MONEY TO END UP AT THE END OF THE MONTH IN THE POSITIVE.

woohoo.") They only have $40 available per day, and they are in the hole $55? So their available amount is negative $15.00.

Example:

$40 / day						
Sun 4	**Mon** 5	**Tues** 6	**Wed**	**Thurs** 8	**Fri** 9	**Sat** 10
A: $40	**A:** $40	**A:** $80	**A:** ($15)	**A:**	**A:**	**A:**
U: ($40)	**U:** $0	**U:** ($135)		**U:**	**U:**	**U:**
D: $0	**D:** $40	**D:** ($55)		**D:**	**D:**	**D:**

Mary has been a good soldier, but you know what – she wants that double shot, non-fat, grande vanilla latte. She knows they have no money budgeted to spend on Wednesday, but she really needs that cup of coffee to get her going. She talked with Bill and he is packing his lunch and will not be spending any money that day. So she spends $4.00 at Starbucks – but really disciplines herself the rest of the day to not spend any more money. So now their calendar looks like the following:

$40 / day

Sun 4	**Mon** 5	**Tues** 6	**Wed** 7	**Thurs** 8	**Fri** 9	**Sat** 10
A: $40	**A:** $40	**A:** $80	**A:** ($15)	**A:**	**A:**	**A:**
U: ($40)	**U:** $0	**U:** ($135)	**U:** ($4)	**U:**	**U:**	**U:**
D: $0	**D:** $40	**D:** ($55)	**D:** ($19)	**D:**	**D:**	**D:**

Notice the Difference row is negative $19. Here is how that works – again using simple math. They were in the hole $55. They only have $40 to spend per day. So they are starting off the day negative $15. Because they spend $4, they end the day at negative $19.

Negative $19 added to the next day amount of $40 gives you a positive $21 Available for Thursday the 8th.

Example:

$40 / day							
Sun 4	Mon 5	Tues 6	Wed 7	Thur	Fri 9	Sat 10
A: $40	A: $40	A: $80	A: ($15)	A: $21	A:	A:
U: ($40)	U: $0	U: ($135)	U: ($4)		U:	U:
D: $0	D: $40	D: ($55)	D: ($19)		D:	D:

The calendar continues on like this until the end of the pay period.

The main point in doing this is so that you always know how much money you have to spend each day. If you are in the hole and need to tighten it up for a few days, you will know it. How often do you go through a week not having any idea how much money you have left to spend? My guess is too often. This approach gives you a simple tool to always know where you stand with your money.

Notice, *Winning With Money* is not telling you WHAT you can spend your money on. That is completely up to you.

FOOD BUDGET

I am not sure about you, but I like to eat. My family rips through the food, so we need a separate food budget. So does the Smith family. We identified their food budget number above in Chapter 3, Step 7. The food budget is very simple to follow. You simply keep track of what you spend on food on the same calendar as your Daily Spend. (The calendar you can download will have a space for your food budget.) The Food Budget does not include restaurant meals or other items you might buy at the grocery store, i.e soap, shampoo, cleaners, etc. These belong in your Daily Spend.

In the Smith household, Bill is the grocery shopper. At the start of the week, he went down to the local grocery store to buy a few items. Their weekly budget for food is $100. He ended up spending $55. He will write that amount in the Spent column and also keep a running total.

$40 / day

Sun	4	Mon	5	Tues	6	Wed	7	Thurs	8	Fri	9	Sat	10
A:	$40	A:	$40	A:	$80	A:	($15)	A:	$21	A:		A:	
U:	($40)	U:	$0	U:	($135)	U:	($4)	U:		U:		U:	
D:	$0	D:	$40	D:	($55)	D:	($19)	D:		D:		D:	

FOOD BUDGET	Date	Spent	Total
Sun 4th: $100	1/4	$55	$55
Sun 11th: $100			

Later in the week, Bill again went to the store and this time spent a total of $50 on food on Thursday the 8th. Because this is over what they have budgeted, they should account for it in one of two ways: 1) add the extra amount to their Used row on the Daily Spend calendar or 2) subtract the amount from the following week's food budget. In this example, we will use option number 1. So, in this case, they have $100 budgeted for the week and they end up spending $105. $5 will be added to the Used amount on the 8th.

$40 / day							
Sun 4	**Mon** 5	**Tues** 6	**Wed** 7	**Thurs** 8	**Fri** 9	**Sat** 10
A: $40	A: $40	A: $80	A: ($15)	A: $21	A: $56	A:
U: ($40)	U: $0	U: ($135)	U: ($4)	U: ($5)		U:
D: $0	D: $40	D: ($55)	D: ($19)	D: $16		D:

FOOD BUDGET

Sun 4th: $100

Sun 11th: $100

Date	Spent	Total
1/4	$55	$55
1/8	$50	$105

The following Sunday, they have a brand new food budget to use for the new week.

Now, let's assume they spent LESS than their budget for food. They would simply add the amount they have left over from their food budget to their food budget for the next week.

I also know folks who simply leave the extra funds alone and save that amount at the end of the month, or use to fill in the gaps on their Daily Spend budget if needed.

GASOLINE

The final piece of the calendar is the Gas Budget. It works the exact same way as the Food Budget. It will also be added into the calendar you can download on the same page.

As we mentioned, Bill drives a good distance to work each day, so they have a separate gas budget. On Monday the 5th, Bill needed to buy gas on his way to work. Gas is expensive, so fortunately he has a separate amount of money set aside to fill up his tank. Their gas budget is $62.50 per week. (Bill drives a fuel efficient car – smart dude.) He spends $45 and it lasts him all week. He can then add the extra $17.50 to their budget for the following week. Or, like the food budget, they can save the extra amount, or use to fill in the gaps on their Daily Spend budget.

$40 / day

Sun	4	Mon	5	Tues	6	Wed	7	Thurs	8	Fri	9	Sat	10
A:	$40	A:	$40	A:	$80	A:	($15)	A:	$21	A:	$56	A:	
U:	($40)	U:	$0	U:	($135)	U:	($4)	U:	($5)	U:		U:	
D:	$0	D:	$40	D:	($55)	D:	($19)	D:	$16	D:		D:	

FOOD BUDGET	Date	Spent	Total
Sun 4th: $100	1/4	$55	$55
	1/8	$50	$105
Sun 11th: $100			

GAS BUDGET	Date	Spent	Total
Sun 4th: $62.50	1/5	$45	$45
Sun 11th: $80			

Now, let's say Bill and Mary spent more than their budgeted amount, say $75 on gas for the week. They should account for it in one of two ways: 1) add the extra amount to their Used row on the Daily Spend calendar or 2) subtract the amount from the following week's gas budget. *We will demonstrate option 2 this time.* In your case, it is important to be flexible. You know your situation. It is going to be different for everyone. For the example below, we will simply subtract it from the next week's gas budget.

FOOD BUDGET	Date	Spent	Total
Sun 4th: $100	1/4	$55	$55
	1/8	$50	$105
Sun 11th: $100			

GAS BUDGET	Date	Spent	Total
Sun 4th: $62.50	1/5	$75	$75
Sun 11th: $50			

Don't be intimidated by this process. This exercise uses simple math you learned in grade school. Nothing complicated. **_The hardest part is actually sitting down and doing it._** WinningWithMoney.com is designed to help you build out your calendar with as little effort as possible. It will take some work, but the rewards will be well worth your efforts.

Chapter 5 will address many of the questions you might have about building your calendar and determining your Daily Spend figure.

4

QUESTIONS:

1)   Are you effectively communicating with your spouse (or with yourself) on what you spend?

2)   What special circumstances in your life will need to be accounted for in building your calendar?

MANAGING YOUR CALENDAR

This is a process that WILL take some tweaking to get right. In fact, I can almost guarantee that you will need to tweak and adjust your budget numerous times the first couple of months using this system. And that's OK. That is exactly what you should be doing. Communicate with your spouse on what is working and what is not working. Do you need more on the food budget? How about the gas budget? Is the Daily Spend too much, just right or something else…?

A few thoughts on going through this process:

MY DAILY SPEND IS PRETTY SMALL?

Now that you have gone through this exercise, you should have an amount to live on – hopefully. If not, then you need to go back and analyze your situation.

First, look at your fixed costs. Are there areas you could cut back on? Dropping certain "luxuries" is not the most fun thing in the world, but can certainly free up some cash if you need it.

1)   Satellite or Cable? Do you need the Premium Plus package? Really?

2)   Do you still need that telephone land line?

Many people are going with just their cell phone.

3) Is there a cheaper cell phone package you could go with?

4) Do you really need to pay someone to mow your grass?

5) Could you wash and iron your own clothes?

6) Is your air conditioner turned down too low – or your heat too high?

7) Do you still get the daily newspaper?

8) How much are you spending on your gym membership? (Get outside – it's more fun anyway.)

9) Starbucks – or brew your own at home?

10) Bottled water versus tap water?

> AGAIN, THERE ARE COUNTLESS DOLLARS TO BE SAVED WHEN YOU REALLY PUT SOME THOUGHT INTO WHAT YOU NEED AND DON'T NEED.

Again, there are countless dollars to be saved when you really put some thought into what you need and don't need. If you have the cash – great. But if not, there are almost always places to pull back your spending.

Second, take a look at your Food Budget and Gas Budget. With your Food Budget, there is almost always ways to cut back on your spending. If you really like to eat good food and not cut back in this area – then don't. Find other areas to cut back on. However, if your budget is tight and you don't have a lot of room to slash, the Food Budget is one area where you can find excess. It might not be "The Food Channel" at your house each night, but there are ways to eat very healthy and inexpensively if your funds are tight.

1) If you are eating a lot of packaged foods and pre-made meals, you most certainly have some room to cut. Learn how to cook and watch your food budget go much further.

2) Learn to cook using whole foods. Not only will your food taste better, the cost is much more affordable.

3) Clip coupons. At WinningWithMoney.com, we contain links to a variety of websites dedicated to helping you become the most efficient and thrifty shopper possible.

4) Consider changing where you shop to a discount grocer. Big box "club" stores are awesome places – but absolute budget killers. Unless you are a small business owner, it doesn't make financial sense to do most of your shopping at these places. Most people that walk in there come out with at least a $100 tab and end up buying something they really didn't need in the first place.

"It was SUCH a good deal – it was stupid not to buy it." Yeah, OK.

5)   Think pasta.

The Gas Budget is a little bit trickier. Think about carpooling – or if you live in a metro area, consider walking, riding a bike or using public transportation. Not only will you save on gas, you will save on parking charges. And, you are helping clean the air – always a good thing.

Last, look at your income. Is there any income you are leaving out of the equation that you could be adding back in? Some questions to consider:

1)   Are you saving too much cash each month?

2)   Are you saving too much in your 401K or IRA?

3)   What other automatic withdrawals are coming out?

4)   Could you increase your deductions to keep more of your tax dollars?

THERE ARE COUNTLESS DRAINS ON YOUR PAYCHECK EACH MONTH. TAKE INVENTORY AND MAKE EVERY DOLLAR COUNT FOR SOMETHING.

OK...I DID ALL THAT - NOW WHAT?

If you have done all these things and you are still not coming up with a positive *Winning With Money* figure, you need to think about some more dramatic changes. Start thinking about how you can generate more income:

1) Is there a promotion or chance to improve your income at work?

2) Is there a possibility of taking on an additional job?

3) If your spouse is not working, could that be an option?

4) Are their things you can sell to generate some short-term income until you find a more permanent fix?

Another idea to think about is perhaps selling your home and moving into one with a cheaper mortgage. Again, this is not a fun thing to consider, but a choice that could dramatically change your financial picture. I will discuss how much home a person should buy in Chapter 7.

When times are tight – get creative. If you've read this far – you are clearly committed to making things better in your financial life. It will take some hard work and some sacrifice, but it will be worth it when you come out the other side. I promise.

I WORK ON COMMISSION - NOW WHAT?

Many folks reading this book are working on commission. Excellent. I do as well. If there is one thing that I have learned – it is this: There are good months and there are tough months.

If your income fluctuates on a month-to-month basis, I recommend you do a few things. First, go through the process and identify your fixed costs, gas budget, and food budget.

Then, calculate your Daily Spend using your average income over 12 months. This will give you a set amount that you know you need to live on.

Now, I recommend creating a separate account in which you put excess money in on your good months. This is an account in which you draw from in months where your income does not meet your fixed costs. Simply transfer the cash from that account to your main account to cover your fixed costs and spending cash. THIS WILL TAKE DISCIPLINE. It will only work if you take excess money in your good months and put that in your separate account to draw from when you have a bad month. If you do this, you should be able to create stability in meeting your monthly obligations.

WHERE DO I KEEP THE CALENDAR?

Remember the story I told in the introduction of this book? We keep our calendar on the fridge. I like to eat – so do my kids. We keep the calendar in the most used, visible spot in our entire house - the fridge. My wife and I are constantly in or around the fridge throughout the day and we are forced to view our budget. Not that I want to be thinking about money all day – but I am reminded each time I am in the kitchen what we have available to spend that day. It gives us a reminder to discuss with each other upcoming events that might need extra cash. It prompts us to update the calendar on a daily basis.

Maybe your bathroom mirror is a good spot. Viewing and thinking about your budget first thing in the morning might be a good habit to get into. If you and your spouse get ready at the same time each morning, this could be a perfect spot.

Perhaps at your place of work or in your car would work best. If you are computer person and love to have everything electronic – do that. It is really up to you. Remember – do what works for you and your family. Put the calendar wherever it takes to keep you up to date and in the know.

> YOU CAN BEGIN TO START MAKING YOUR DREAMS HAPPEN.

I SEEM TO HAVE EXTRA CASH?

Good problem to have! **The truth is, when you discipline yourself and pay attention to your money, you will probably have excess cash.** That is the goal. You can begin to start making your dreams happen. We will discuss some ideas in the coming chapters on some intelligent choices for your extra cash.

First and foremost, if you have extra cash, increase the amount you save each month instead of spending more each month.

COMMUNICATION

Like many things in life, communication is critical when managing your money. Managing your money will help you communicate more effectively.

By having an agreed upon budget, you can eliminate many of the problems couples have with their finances. Nearly every statistic claims the number one stressor on a marriage is finances. And for good reason. If you fail to have a plan and a tool to which you both agree, finances can be a tricky, complicated and messy subject. It's often relegated to the "don't bring it up" category and things only spiral downhill from there.

This method can help you and your family get on the same page and work together to achieve your goals and aspirations.

**If you are a single person – learning how to communicate honestly with yourself is just as important.

KEEP IT SIMPLE. KEEP IT FUN.

Please remember that this whole exercise is designed to help you have more success in your financial life. This is not a hard system and certainly not a rigid one. It is supposed to help you communicate, think and ultimately save you time and money.

This is not an exact science. Be flexible. If you find new categories and new budget items that work for you – use them. Experiment, be flexible, debate, think, argue and challenge. MAKE THIS SYSTEM YOUR SYSTEM.

I am excited for you. Good luck and be sure to keep us informed of your progress at WinningWithMoney.com.

> *THE SECRET TO WINNING IS CONSTANT,*
> *CONSISTENT MANAGEMENT.*
> *- TOM LANDRY*

5

QUESTIONS:

1) If you are bit short on your Daily Spend figure – what can you cut?
2) If you have some excess cash – how much can you increase your savings rate?
3) Where will you keep your calendar?

#1. **All good things in life require simple disciplines. Money is no different.**

This plan will not work if you are not committed to some simple disciplines outlined within these chapters. In fact, no financial plan will work without executing simple disciplines. **If this plan is not right for you – no problem. Continue to search for one that is.** But know this – good money management begins with a choice to make things better. If you truly make that choice, you will discipline yourself to make it happen.

#2. **All good things in life require simple communication. Money is no different.**

If you are married, it is impossible to win with money if you are not on the same page. This is something that must be built together and with an open mind. If you are single, learn to communicate with yourself. Be honest with yourself. Pretending you have more money than you actually possess does not work for very long.

POINTS

Understand that there will be challenges.

Fight through them.

Get tough.

Get creative.

Be flexible.

Be supportive.

YOU CAN WIN. YOU CAN DO THIS.
MAKE THIS A PRIORITY
AND YOU WILL SUCCEED.

WINNING WITH MONEY

BUILDING YOUR EMERGENCY FUND

If there is anything the financial debacle of 2007 through 2009 has taught us – is that we, as individuals and families, need to plan for the worst. Expect the best, (I am always the optimist) but plan for the worst.

Our country continues to feel the effects of high unemployment. It's painful. If you have not lost your job – chances are good that you know someone who has. If you are a new graduate coming out of college, you are well aware of the employment challenges facing your newly anointed class.

Unfortunately, hardships also come in other forms. Major medical emergencies. Accidents. Divorce. Family trouble. The list can go on for pages. Things happen and we have no way of knowing they are going to occur. Unfortunately, things strike when we are least expecting. The point is this – we need to have a fall back, a way out – when difficulties occur. Too often, Americans turn to various forms of debt to assist them when things get ugly. Home equity lines, credit cards and payday loans can wipe out your net worth and drive you into serious debt problems.

This is where an emergency fund becomes essential. An emergency fund is cash you have set aside for the ugly times in your life. This is cash that you simply, never, ever touch – unless you are forced to due to an emergency. Traditional wisdom says to keep three to six months worth of your average expenses. I think it is important to take it a step further.

In chapter 3, we discussed the importance of outlining your monthly fixed expenses in determining your budget. I recommend having an emergency fund that can cover six full months of your expenses plus your daily budget. Nine months would be ideal.

Why six to nine months versus three? The past couple of years have taught us that you can't have too much socked away for difficult times. It is taking people who have lost their jobs on average six months to find new employment. If a medical emergency hits – it becomes even more important to have cash stored away. Medical bills have bankrupted millions of Americans. The trend is only going to get steeper.

Let's go back to Bill and Mary for moment as an example of what their emergency fund would look like. In chapter three, their fixed monthly expenses turned out to be $2,065. They also determined their Food, Gas and *Winning With Money* amount to be $1,765. *(We can eliminate their savings amount from this figure. It is safe to assume a person living off savings is not going to be saving money at this point.)* In their case, if they add those two amounts together, they have a monthly figure that they need to live on.

Because Bill and Mary are HUGE believers in the

Emergency Fund, they worked hard to build up their fund to a full nine months. That gives them a figure of $34,470. *(Six months would be $22,980.)* That might seem like a lot. And hopefully it is. Emergencies can be very expensive ordeals.

What are the benefits to having a well-funded emergency fund?

1) It is always better to borrow on yourself versus the bank. When borrowing on yourself, you don't incur interest fees, loan fees, late fees or "we the bank - need more money from you" fees.

> IT IS ALWAYS BETTER TO BORROW ON YOURSELF VERSUS THE BANK.

2) My grandfather is a chiseled veteran of World War II and a son of the Great Depression. He is a man who doesn't mince words and tells it like he sees it. He worked very hard in his life and put himself in a position of financial freedom. He used to call his emergency fund the "Go to Hell Fund" (GTH). Why is that Grandpa? "So that anytime, anywhere – I can tell the boss to go to hell and not worry about paying the mortgage." Good stuff Grandpa.

3) Good old fashioned Peace. When you have a cushion to fall on – it doesn't hurt when you fall. When you have money in the bank – socked away for the proverbial rainy day – you sleep easier at night.

I would recommend keeping your emergency fund in a bank account you can access at any time without penalty. There are numerous options you can choose from: money market accounts, savings accounts, online bank accounts. DO NOT put your emergency fund into a CD. CD's often carry penalties for breaking the term in which you committed too. That totally defeats the purpose of having an accessible emergency fund.

I personally recommend keeping your emergency fund in a high interest savings account. These accounts pay CD style interest rates, along with other benefits, without having a penalty associated with early withdrawal. Not only that – you earn interest on your money that will grow and accrue over time – helping pad your emergency fund even deeper.

Most of these types of accounts are available at your local community banks and credit unions. I recommend opening one of these high interest savings accounts with a quality, local banking institution that: a) you trust, b) is readily accessible, and c) is tied to a free or reward checking account that will allow for the easy transfer of funds if ever needed. A good place to start in locating these types of accounts can be found at www.checkingfinder.com.

6

QUESTIONS:

1)   Do you have an emergency fund in place today?

2)   Can you think of any good reasons to not have
             an emergency fund?

UNDERSTANDING DEBT

There's an old banker's adage that says:

> "Borrow to buy things that appreciate.
> Save to buy things that depreciate."

I guess that is really old advice because that is certainly not our society's mentality on debt today. It is common-place for people to borrow to buy ANYTHING they feel like, whenever they feel like.

I am not going to beat the anti-debt drum like some folks, but I will make some very important observations about debt. Going back to our old banker's adage, let's discuss the difference between good debt and bad debt. First, the good debt.

GOOD DEBT...

Borrowing money to buy things that appreciate is usually a good principle if you don't have the cash to buy it outright. (Appreciate in this context means the purchase you make goes up in value.) The principle is predicated on buying things within reason and within your realm of affordability. What things appreciate?

HOME OWNERSHIP

Home ownership is generally a good thing. The increase in the value of the home is called equity. Of course there will be times when the housing market falls, sometimes precipitously (2007 to 2009), so you need a time horizon of ownership that will allow you to build equity even if the housing market depreciates over the short term. Real estate in most years will be worth more each year compared to the prior year. Building equity in a home is a smart move for a number of reasons:

1)   It is always better to pay into something you will potentially own, versus paying someone else's ownership, i.e. rent.

2)   Owning a home gives a person a sense of responsibility and self worth.

3)   For tax reasons, home ownership can help you lower your taxable income each year. And that is always a good thing.

However, many, many Americans make the mistake of

borrowing TOO much money to buy a home. If Bill and Mary are making $75,000 a year, they should not be thinking of buying a home that costs $500,000. The mortgage payment will end up paralyzing the rest of their income. **Most experts will advise you to never have a mortgage more than 25% of your take home pay.**

When I say most, I mean most reputable lenders. Some lenders during the 2000's pushed the limits way past what they should have been. I know of some people who bought and refinanced homes and were given enough leeway to buy a home that would have cost them up to 42% of their take home income each month. That means that 42% of their take home pay would be going to pay for their home each month. That is WAY too much. It is because of this that many homeowners are now struggling to pay their mortgage. If it is a stretch when times are good, it is almost impossible when times are rough.

> MOST EXPERTS WILL ADVISE YOU TO NEVER HAVE A MORTGAGE MORE THAN 25% OF YOUR TAKE HOME PAY.

Let's look into this a step further. Bill and Mary have worked hard and want to move into a nicer home. They have two kids and are starting to feel a little pinched in their current confines. They have talked with many lenders and have been given enough room to buy a home with a mortgage that is going to be about 24% of their take home income. Because this is such a priority for them, they are comfortable with this amount.

However, it does mean some changes for them. They will probably not be able to afford the gym membership and the lawn care service anymore. (That's OK; generic fertilizer and push-ups will suffice until they generate additional income.) That is one of the great things about living in America: people get to choose what they need and what they do not need to make great things happen in their lives.

Let's say Bill and Mary receive a raise and earn $80,000 per year and take home $60,000 after tax, savings and other deductions. If we apply the rule of not borrowing more than 25% of their take-home pay to purchase a home:

25% of $60,000 is $15,000.

If we divide the $15,000 by 12 months, we get $1,250.

Bill and Mary should not have a mortgage payment that exceeds $1,250 per month. Anything more than this will make Bill and Mary "house poor." House poor is a term used to describe a person who scrapes everything they have together each month just to make the mortgage payment – leaving them with little money to do anything else.

The bank might sell you on the notion that you can afford to own a $1 million dollar home – but that does not mean it is the smart thing to do. (This was a primary contributor to the economic crash the entire world experienced in 2007-2009.) Bankers enticed buyers to finance homes they had no business getting into. They gave them easy credit with very little thought as to what would happen if they couldn't make the mortgage payment. And as we discussed earlier in the book, people lose jobs, get sick, miss payments, etc... The moral of the story is simply this: Only finance things you can REALISTICALLY afford to make payments on.

EDUCATION

I am a firm believer in education. It is very difficult to expand on one's dreams without sufficient education. I am not just talking college; it could be trade schools, certifications, etc... Some people have the cash to pay for their education. It might come from years of hard work. Perhaps a family sacrificed for years to help their loved ones go to school. For most people though, financing their education is the only option.

If you have to finance your education – be smart about it. Just like owning a home, don't run out and get a financing package just because you can. Look at all the options, calculate exactly what you need, and determine if the return is worth it. What do I mean by "worth it?"

> IF YOU HAVE TO FINANCE YOUR EDUCATION – BE SMART ABOUT IT.

I know many people who took on enormous amounts of "student aid" to get a college degree, only to be mired in a sea of debt payments that are as big as a mortgage. They have no hope of paying them back anytime soon. **If you decide to take on debt to pay for school, make** *sure the degree in which you seek will allow you to pay back your debt load.* Financing an education to Harvard to become a teacher probably isn't a good idea. There is nothing wrong with becoming a teacher, but teachers don't make a lot of money. Most teachers are not going to make a high enough income to make payments on a Harvard-sized debt. "But doctors take on huge debt to go to medical school." Yep, they sure do. But they end up getting paid handsomely for their efforts when they become doctors and can afford to pay the debt back. Again, be smart in what you choose to finance.

There are many good things to borrow money for. But beware of the consequences. The Bible states in Proverbs 22:7 "...the borrower is servant to the lender." Ask anyone who is knee deep in debt what that means and they will gladly help you understand.

> *Challenge:*
> I would also encourage those thinking about higher education to consider the option of going about it debt free. Though difficult, it is entirely possible to complete college or trade school without taking on debt. It will most likely require tough sacrifices and late nights. I would encourage anyone energized about this challenge to check out *Debt Free U*, by Zac Bissonnette. This book advises ways to complete a degree without the burden of borrowing money.

My favorite boss and good friend completed a four year degree from a Wisconsin university without taking a single nickel from his family – or a bank. He worked night jobs, morning jobs, studied hard and ate a lot of ramen noodles – but he did it. He is the first to tell you that the principles he learned through that experience made him tougher, more balanced and ultimately, very successful in his later years.

BAD DEBT...

Now, the bad debt. Or should I say, the popular debt. Americans love to buy whatever they want right now. "Forget saving man – give it to me now." "I got credit. My limit is high enough. Let's party!" Yeah, party right to bankruptcy.

Borrowing money to buy things that depreciate is not a good idea. In fact, it's a really dumb idea. The basic principle of saving runs so contrary to popular opinion, but lies at the heart of America's personal finance problem.

"But I really need that nice car to get to work." Really? Do you? Automobiles are a depreciating asset. (Depreciating in this context means that the item purchased loses value each second of the day that passes.) Cars may be a fact of life, but that does not mean you have to borrow money to have one. If you save up and want to buy a really cool car – awesome! Do it! But if you don't have the money to pay for a really cool car – buy a used, reliable car for a fraction of the price and save for the one you really want. By the time you are done saving, the car you really wanted will then be much cheaper.

Americans also buy boats, motorcycles, RV's, ATV's, snowmobiles, etc all on credit. Again – these are quickly sinking ships. They all lose money every day they sit in your garage. There is nothing wrong with having any of these things (I am saving for a boat as I write this, more on that later) – but pay cash for them. You will never regret it.

I was in a hotel lobby having breakfast the other day, enjoying my standard "on-the-road" early morning cuisine of two yogurts, one banana and a glass of apple juice. I noticed the TV was tuned in to a popular morning news show. The host was interviewing a "finance" expert on summer vacations. The tag line in the backdrop of the interview was this: "How to Pay Off Your Summer Vacation in Three Months!"

Hmmm, here is an "expert" on probably the most popular morning show on the planet, and she is telling viewers "smart" ways to "pay off" your vacation in three months. Would it not make more sense for a so called "expert" to advise people on how to "save" for the vacation they want in three months and not have to worry about paying it off? Think about it. How much more fun would you have if you actually had money in the bank to pay for the cool vacation you want to take. I guarantee you the fun, relaxation and adventures will be much more fulfilling. The genius of financial independence means freedom and flexibility – never forget that!

CREDIT CARDS

The last point I will make on debt is credit cards. If you have them, pay the balance off each month. Paying only the minimum balance will drive your debt deeper and deeper into a hole you might never climb out of. If you have multiple cards, get down to one. **Try not to use them at all. Credit cards get people into deep trouble, very quickly.**

I am not going to cite all the statistics about credit cards and why they are such a drain on our society today. If you are reading this book, there is a good chance you know that. So do this: Look yourself in the mirror – really look – and ask yourself if you really need to use your credit card today. If you really have to have that new jacket paid for with your Visa. If you really need to eat at that nice restaurant paid for with MasterCard. If the answer is yes, then do it. But I bet it's probably a better idea to wear your old jacket and eat at home.

> *A simple tactic:*
> Bill and Mary keep their credit cards frozen in a
> zip lock bag of water in their freezer. If they really
> need the stuff they want to buy on credit– they are
> forced to think about it in advance – making darn
> sure that is a choice they want to make.

SUSTAINABILITY?

Sustainability is a big buzzword right now in our culture. And for good reason. It simply means doing more with the resources we have available to us – and not wasting resources we really don't need to waste. People don't really think of debt and sustainability in the same measure. But think about it – the two are completely intertwined. Much of the consumerism and wasteful spending throughout the world is caused by people buying things they don't really need. Sure, they want it – but do they really need it? It is the "want it" mentality that has created the amazing debt loads of so many individuals. And in the same context, the "want it" mentality has created much of the wastefulness of our resources.

Is there a good reason to have 10 different winter coats in the closet? Is there a reason for a family of three to have four vehicles? Is there a good reason to buy a XXL-gigabyte iPhone to replace the nine-month-old XL gigabyte iPhone? If so, and you have the cash to do it, then go for it. But most of the time, there is not a good reason, and people don't have the cash. People buy things they can't afford with money they don't have. That is the least sustainable practice of all. Something to think about…

7

QUESTIONS:

1) What is your good debt?
2) What is your bad debt? How fast can you get rid of it?
3) Are you a "wasteful" spender?

    How can you be a more "responsible" spender?

INVESTMENTS

Investing can be a delicate subject. This is not an investment strategy book, so I am certainly not going to dive into the many possible opinions on where you need to invest your money. But I will provide you with some advice that might help.

First and foremost, smart investing starts with setting financial goals. It is impossible to have an investment strategy without having goals to shoot for. A sound and well thought out investment strategy can help you achieve those goals. Sit down with your spouse, a mentor, whoever, and talk through what you want to achieve and in what time frame. It might be something as simple as owning your first home within five years. It may be a complex business plan you hope to implement within three years. Whatever it is, dedicate some time to thinking through it and talking with people you trust. (We will discuss more about goal setting in Chapter 11.)

Bill and Mary have a goal to send both of their kids to college. Both Bill and Mary paid their own way through college and while it was a great challenge and character builder – they want their kids to have a different experience. (Both sides of that argument have merit – but that is a different discussion for a different day.)

Bill and Mary really have no experience with investments and don't have a good starting place. It is important that they find an expert to help provide a solid and sound strategy.

FINDING THE
RIGHT EXPERT
CAN HELP YOU
ACCOMPLISH
YOUR GOALS.

Finding the right expert can help you accomplish your goals. Experts come in many shapes and sizes: bankers, CPA's, lawyers, financial advisors, insurance people, etc... Here are some keys to finding an expert.

1. Most importantly, find someone you trust. Someone you can really talk with and who will level with you. A person who will give you sound advice - even if it's advice you don't want to hear.

2. Someone who takes interest in more than just your money – who generally cares about you and your family's well being.

Many things can happen over the course of your life – you want to make sure the person who is advising you knows about your different life situations and will be there if something drastic takes place.

3. Find an advisor that shares your principles and ideas. If you are a person that believes in giving back to your community – then find an advisor that also shares that belief. Having someone who shares similar standards can open your eyes to new and different investment possibilities you may never have thought of.

4. If the advisor you have selected charges a fee for their services – make darn sure you know exactly how much that fee is and what it is going to cost you each month. If the expert you choose is unable to provide you with a really close estimate – you need to find a new expert.

5. Make sure the person advising you is smart, intelligent, well connected and well read. Just because your neighbor is a good guy and a CPA does not mean he is a good tax advisor. Just because you go to church with a local banker does not mean she is a quality banker. Do your

homework. Spend the time needed to determine if the person you want to advise you really is an expert.

That may seem like a difficult set of criteria – and it is. It's supposed to be.   (Hint: Finding an expert is not going to happen when watching golf on TV on a Sunday afternoon.) We've spent the whole book talking about how to better spend our money and stay out of debt. The last thing we want to do is hire some nut job to mismanage the efforts of our hard work. Be disciplined, take the time, have the conversations, and watch your net worth grow.

8

QUESTIONS:

1)   What is your investment philosophy?

2)   Who are the experts you trust? Why?

NET WORTH:
WHAT'S THAT?

Most people I talk with today have no concept of what their net worth is. And why would they? Isn't that something wealthy people worry about? The quick answer is yes; wealthy people in general do know what their net worth is. But there is no reason that you shouldn't know it as well.

In its simplest terms, net worth is calculated by adding up everything you *own* and subtracting everything you *owe*. In the business world, it's simply a balance sheet: your assets should equal your liabilities plus equity.

Let's look at Bill and Mary for example:

What Bill and Mary own:

Home Value:	$300,000
401K:	$20,000
Savings Account:	$10,000
Emergency Fund:	$30,000
Vehicle worth:	$7,000
TOTAL:	$367,000

What Bill and Mary owe:

Mortgage (principal left):	$200,000
Car loan:	$2,000

Credit Card Debt:	$3,000
Student Loan:	$5,000
TOTAL:	$210,000

Net Worth: $367,000 minus $210,000 equals $157,000.

Bill and Mary have a net worth of $157,000.

FIGURING YOUR NET WORTH

Figuring out your net worth is much easier than it might sound. I have included a resource on www. WinningWithMoney.com for you to download and fill out yourself. The worksheet on the opposite page and again in the back of the book are also included as resources to help you work through this exercise.

SO WHY DO I NEED TO KNOW MY NET WORTH?

WHEN THE SKY STARTS FALLING, YOU WANT TO HAVE A GOOD IDEA OF WHERE YOUR SHELTERS ARE.

Knowing your net worth gives you a very clear picture of where you stand in your financial life and where you need to spend some time adjusting. It can give you a clear understanding of your asset mix as well. Perhaps you are overly concentrated in cash. Maybe you are heavy in real estate. Perhaps you are deep into stocks and need to re-balance. Given the financial disaster that took place in 2008 and 2009 – this is good information to have. When the sky starts falling, you want to have a good idea of where your shelters are. Knowing your net worth allows you to stay financially balanced.

NET WORTH WORKSHEET
Date (update quarterly): ___ / ___ / ___
Net Worth Goal: $_____

ASSETS (What you OWN)

Home Value	$_____
Retirement Account 1	$_____
Retirement Account 2	$_____
Stocks 1	$_____
Stocks 2	$_____
Education 1	$_____
Education 2	$_____
Savings 1	$_____
Savings 2	$_____
Checking	$_____
Medical	$_____
Vehicle 1	$_____
Vehicle 2	$_____
Vehicle 3	$_____
Other	$_____
Other	$_____
TOTAL ASSETS	$_____

LIABILITIES (What you OWE)

Home Mortgage	$_____
Unpaid Taxes	$_____
Car Debt 1	$_____
Car Debt 2	$_____
Credit Card Debt	$_____
Student Loans	$_____
Other	$_____
TOTAL LIABILITIES	$_____

NET WORTH (*OWN* minus *OWE*):

Another important reason to know your net worth is in the unfortunate event of a family emergency. If something happens to you or your spouse – you will want those closest to you to know what your financial picture looks like.

Perhaps a family member or close friend has a terrible accident and you want to know if you have the resources to help. Taking a look at your net worth sheet will give you a clear understanding of your ability to help.

I recommend updating your net worth sheet on a quarterly basis. Some folks might find it helpful to update monthly, some annually. Whatever you decide to do, keep track of your progress. Keep a copy of each statement you build in a file and watch your net worth grow. If it's going the opposite way – seek out a professional and figure out what to do to change it up. By having this process completed, you will have a much more powerful discussion with the experts who are working with you.

9

QUESTIONS:

1)   What's your net worth?

2)   Do you feel you are balanced?
     What are you going to do about it?

GIVING BACK

The American culture is one of the most, if not THE most giving cultures in the world today. Whether it is to a charity, a cause, a relief effort, an educational entity or a church, Americans are generous with their money and their time. I truly believe a strong society depends on the generosity of its people.

FAMILY DECISION

Giving money to certain entities and causes should be a family decision. What values are important to your family? What events are happening in the world that are drawing your attention? What are things in your community that your kids are involved with or concerned about? Engaging your children helps them learn that the world does not revolve around them and will help them understand at an early age an important concept. The notion of giving back helps accomplish a number of things. I will outline three:

STAYING BALANCED

People tend to lose sight of the big picture when they spend money only on themselves. Giving is not a "religious thing" or an "obligation thing" – it's a people thing. When we give, we gain a sense of a larger picture – that life is not just about us and the things we want to accomplish, but about helping others meet basic needs and giving them a chance at accomplishing their dreams and goals. The wealthiest people in America have countless foundations and funds set up to help others throughout the world. In a much smaller way, common folks like you and I can do the same thing: by budgeting our money and managing our finances with solid principles, we too can participate in helping others live better lives.

> BY MANAGING OUR FINANCES WITH SOLID PRINCIPLES, WE TOO CAN PARTICIPATE IN HELPING OTHERS LIVE BETTER LIVES.

SPEND LESS

People who give on a regular basis tend to stay out of debt and spend less money on things they simply don't need. They are typically good at managing their money and very responsible in their purchasing habits. I truly believe this is because they have set their focus not on accumulating stuff, but on being good citizens and helping others. There is certainly nothing wrong with having nice things and rewarding yourself for a well-earned effort. However, consider using a portion of your gains to help others. You will most likely never regret it.

CONNECTED TO YOUR COMMUNITY

When people give back, they almost always have a stronger sense of their place in the community. Some people give for recognition. That's not what I am talking about and I think most are not that way. People feel more connected because they are personally vested in a positive outcome of a cause. You would not give to the Special Olympics and hope the organization fails. You would give and wish them the best. By investing in and giving back to solid organizations – you are contributing to a better community – a better world.

SO, HOW MUCH SHOULD YOU GIVE?

This is an excellent question and one that has no right answer. It is very dependent on many factors. The bottom line – it is a personal decision. Only you and your family can make that decision. Don't feel pressured by an outside influence. Only after pounding through the aforementioned exercises of knowing how much you spend, setting your budget and determining your net worth will you truly be able to make a solid decision about how much to give.

After going through the exercise – you might determine that you have no money to give at all. And that's OK. Going through the process will set you on a path to be able to give in the future. Part of giving is giving responsibly. If you don't have the money to give, don't give it. Some people drive themselves deep into debt because they are giving away money they don't have. This is not a good idea.

A couple of examples that have inspired me:

THE ACCOUNTANT

A friend of mine is an entrepreneur who started an accounting firm of sorts. Before starting his company, he worked for a large international consulting company traveling the world and making some good money. He and his wife made a decision to give back $1 for every $1 they saved, up to 10% of his income. So if they saved $100 in a month, they would give $100 that month. When I asked him why he gave back – he told me it kept him less greedy and financially and mentally balanced.

When my friend started his company, he didn't make any money in the beginning. Because he was not making any money and pulling from his savings account each month, their family stopped giving. This is exactly what they should have done. It would have been irresponsible for them to give away money they didn't have. Every bit of extra cash they had went into starting their business and feeding their family.

His company is now very successful and they are giving regularly back to their community and other causes. My point in telling this story is to illustrate that giving is a dynamic exercise. It will and should change each month if you decide to give. Find the right formula for your family.

THE DAD

My kids were recently attending a summer camp in our neighborhood. The camp was organized by volunteers and focused on the kids becoming better citizens. The part of the camp the kids really got into was helping an organization provide wheelchairs for people who could not otherwise afford them. They talked with people in wheelchairs and learned of the valuable importance that chair plays in their lives.

Each night, at the end of camp, the volunteers would encourage the kids to be as generous as possible in helping the organization raise enough money to pay for 20 wheel-chairs. (This really cool company makes their wheelchairs using old mountain bike tires and plastic chairs. They provide chairs for people around the world at a cost of $60 each.)

The camp organized the girls versus boys in the giving competition. By Wednesday of the camp, the giving competition became the most important part of the day for the kids. They were pumped about helping people (and beating the others at giving!)

One night, one little girl came home and told her dad about the cool wheelchair competition at camp. The little girl was so excited. Not about the games, the learning or the friends – she was excited about being able to help someone in need. This little girl was so pumped up – the dad needed to see for himself what was going on. The next day, the dad went to camp with the little girl to see what she was so excited about. The dad was touched by what he saw – but mostly at his little girls determination to help someone. This dad, not a rich man my any means, decided to give his little girl a hundred dollar bill to donate the next night.

Both of my kids came home that night and told me all about this… "little girl who gave $100. Can you believe that!?" I don't know if that dad is a regular "giver" or just someone who was moved to do something extraordinary. But I do know he taught my kids, his little girl and many others in our community that helping others is a pretty great thing.

TRANSPARENCY

Be careful with whom and where you decide to give. Make sure they represent a legitimate organization. Unfortunately, there are many scam artists looking to take advantage of un-suspecting people. Check out the cause on the Internet. Ask the organization for published materials. Never give your debit/credit card information over the phone. Make a requestor send you a form either via email or the mail to make sure they are legitimate. Most genuine organizations will understand this and provide you with the materials needed to make the right decision.

> BE CAREFUL WITH WHOM AND WHERE YOU DECIDE TO GIVE.

Most valid charities and causes have tax exempt status. That simply means that you get to take the amount you gave and reduce it from your taxable income on your taxes for that year. Tax-exempt organizations are most often referred to as 501c-3. This is the tax code the IRS gives to these types of organizations. Always ask for a receipt and keep it in a safe place so you have it available when preparing your tax return the following spring.

I want to again stress that giving is a personal and family decision. There is no "answer" as to how much, how often or if at all. I do know that people who give find it rewarding, it helps them keep the proper perspective in their life and they find it very satisfying to help people in need.

10

QUESTIONS:

1)   If you give, why do you give?

2)   If you don't give – why not?

NOTHING HAPPENS UNLESS FIRST A DREAM.

- CARL SANDBURG

SETTING GOALS

You will miss 100% of the goals you never set. Every time.

We have all heard the importance of setting goals. But few people really sit down and actually set goals. Why? Is it really that hard to do? Is it that we don't want to accomplish things? I believe the answer is simple but tough to admit. Most people don't set goals because they are afraid of failure. "If I set the goal and fail to achieve it – I lose."

LET'S CHANGE THAT MENTALITY RIGHT NOW.

Goal setting does not need to be an arduous task of potential failure. Goal setting needs to be simple, realistic and fun. It also needs to be tactical in nature. Most people that do set goals don't tactically plan on how to achieve them. It is important to strategically set the goal. You then need to outline a plan of what you are going to do – the steps you are going to take (the tactical part) to achieve that goal.

> GOAL SETTING NEEDS TO BE SIMPLE, REALISTIC AND FUN.

KEEP YOUR GOALS SIMPLE

Let's start with keeping them simple. There is no reason to complicate your goals in life. Think about what you would like to accomplish this year. Maybe it is saving for a vacation. Maybe you are looking to spend more time with your kids. Maybe you want to buy a new mountain bike. Awesome, let's start with these three:

Goal #1: Vacation to California

a.   Want to go in July

b.   Save $1,500 for the trip

c.   Cut back on going to out eat the first six month this year to pay for the trip

d.   Research affordable discounts and hotels online

Goal #2: Spend more time with kids

a.   Work less at the office

b.   Work smarter to get home sooner

c.   Get up early to exercise before, not after work

Goal #3: Buy spouse a new bike

a.   Save $1,500

b.   Shop for sales

c.   Lots of research

d.   Buy before May

e.   Cut down on entertainment spending

The goals set above are certainly not complex – rather very achievable. Planning out the action steps to make it happen is the big difference in hitting your goals and coming up short.

Back in chapter 3, we discussed Bill and Mary having a goal of going to Europe to hike and experience the Swiss Alps. We outlined their finances in the previous chapters and know that they now have their numbers under control. Since they implemented *Winning With Money*, they are committing $100 per month to their Swiss Alps Goal. They also save extra money from their Daily Spend when they can. They actually have a goofy picture of a thermometer on their fridge at home charting their progress. (You know, the thermometers you see in a school tracking the latest fund raising goal.)

That is the fun part about setting goals – IT IS YOUR GOAL. It can be whatever you want and you can track it however you want. If a thermometer helps you make it happen – then do it! If it's marbles in a jar, then do it. BUT DO IT. Make it happen and see the results.

SET REALISTIC GOALS

Let's face it; achieving things in life is fun. Our goals should be no different. Set some simple, realistic goals. If you make $30,000 a year and you set a goal to buy a $600,000 house – that is not very realistic. You probably won't make that one. If you weigh 300 pounds and want to lose 150 pounds in three months – you probably won't make that one either. So start off with goals that are attainable and reachable. Look back at the goals above. What are three simple things you want to accomplish this year with your money? Given your current financial picture – are they realistic? Can the budgeting tools and ideas you have learned in this book help you stretch to meet them?

I know some people that set goals so high and so outrageous – they can never achieve them. And that's their point. If they set a goal that is really high – say 50% higher than what it should be, and they only get to 80% of it – then they have actually done 30% better than what they would have done. These are called "stretch goals."

I used to work for a CEO who ran his company by setting stretch goals. It worked very well for him. His company continually pushed the bar higher and higher because of the aggressive nature of the goals that were set. The company never actually hits the goals, but comes darn close each year. By doing so, they achieve far more than they would if the goals were not set so high.

> FIND A GOAL SET-TING STRATEGY THAT WORKS BEST FOR YOU.

But most people don't operate this way. Find a goal setting strategy that works best for you. I recommend starting out with realistic goals and later moving toward "stretch goals" as you gain momentum.

SAVING FOR YOUR GOALS

A great way to hit your savings goals is by allocating a specific amount from each paycheck automatically into a savings account, money market fund or other savings vehicle. I further recommend setting up an account for each goal you have.

Let's say you are saving for three things: 1) A new car to re-place your existing car, 2) a family vacation and 3) a new re-frigerator. Think about setting up an account for each goal. If the money is automatically deducted from your account each paycheck, you don't have the temptation to spend those funds on something else outside of your set goals.

By having separate accounts, you accomplish two main things: 1) It will help keep you motivated toward your goals as you see your accounts grow. 2) It will help you stay honest with yourself and not cheat one goal to accomplish another. If all of your savings are in one big pot, the ten-dency is to start thinking of what you want to buy and have difficulty remembering that $5,000 is for a replacement car, $1000 is for vacation, and $800 is toward a new refrigerator. Having separate accounts will help you achieve success.

Even if you decide not to automate your savings, you can still discipline yourself to put aside money to achieve a goal. One of my fishing pals had a very creative way for saving for a trip to Alaska one year. His business was struggling with the down economy and was not sure he would be able to make our an-nual trip north. He decided he really wanted to go and set a goal to save $1,000 over the course of nine months. His meth-od – a simple envelope in his office drawer. Each paycheck, he pulled a little cash out and put it in the envelope. Each time he went to the store and got change, he put it in the envelope.

I will never forget that day we arrived in Alaska. He pulled out this fat envelope full of random bills and paid our pilot $1,000. Talk about satisfaction. Goal set. Goal achieved. And he did it with nothing but an envelope and will power. It is no coincidence he caught the biggest fish that year… seriously, one of the biggest King Salmon I've ever seen.

MAKE IT FUN!

My last point is that your goals should be fun. Let's not get mired down in the day-to-day personal finance minutia that we forget to have fun! Money should be a resource for us, not a drag. Set some goals that are fun for you – and your family. This is especially important with children in the house. Talk with your family about what they would like to do. Get everyone on board and work on accomplishing the goals together. My family has a goal to buy a ski boat this year. The kids are at the right age, we live near a lake, they love the water – so it makes perfect sense for us.

> MONEY SHOULD BE A RESOURCE FOR US, NOT A DRAG.

We sat down as a family and decided this would be our goal. To achieve this goal, we need to save our money to buy it. The kids have been very focused on this objective. Every time we go to the store they ask if we really need that particular item. If you ask them why they simply respond, "Because that's boat money Dad. Don't waste our boat money." Because we don't finance depreciating assets in our household, we need to save enough cash to buy it outright. What a great way to engage your family and teach them about the importance of saving and budgeting.

You can see that the above discussion inter-mixed both personal and family goals. This is important. Both sets have different purposes. It is important to communicate and discuss your goals to make sure they are simple, realistic and fun. It's also vital from an accountability standpoint. When others know your goals, or you are trying to achieve something as a unit (family, business, team…), everyone holds each other accountable; i.e. "Dad, is that boat money you are spending?"

Have fun with this process. I guarantee your life will be better for it.

Bill and Mary did make it to Europe - a grand slam, two week hiking extravaganza. (They parceled the kids off on their parents for the trip. One set each week. I am not daring enough to write about that part of it…). What makes a vacation even better? Not having to pay for it for years once it is over. Paying cash for something you have dreamed of is SO MUCH more satisfying than going into debt for the same experience. If you haven't tried it, I highly recommend it. You won't regret it!

II

QUESTIONS:
1) 	I challenge you to sit down with your family and set some goals.
2) 	You should seriously do number 1. It's worth it.

READY...SET...GO!

YOU CAN'T BUILD A REPUTATION
ON WHAT YOU ARE GOING TO DO.
- HENRY FORD

IF YOU THINK YOU CAN WIN, YOU CAN WIN.
FAITH IS NECESSARY TO VICTORY.
- WILLIAM HAZLITT

My goal in writing this book was simply to motivate you, provide you with a new tool that can help you manage your money and ultimately make your life better. As I stated earlier in the book, if this method does not work for you – keep searching. Managing your money is so important. If you keep searching, you will find a method and system that works for you and your family.

When I first started writing - as mentioned in the previous chapter - my family had a goal of buying a ski boat. We ended up achieving that goal shortly before this book was finished. (And yes, the book took a while to write – I have a day job.) It took us about 28 months to achieve this goal.

Was it worth it? OH MY! It has been a pure blessing for our family. We were able to find a great boat at a very fair price. If we had bought the boat on credit when we first wanted to, instead of saving to pay cash for, we would have paid considerably more. We set a goal and we did it. No payments, no pressure, no worries.

What's your goal?

What will you accomplish?

GO OUT AND MAKE IT HAPPEN!

One more point I would like to make. No matter how bleak your circumstances appear to be, no matter how bad things are financially – **know this: it can and will get better.** We live in the greatest nation on the face of the earth. No other place in the world gives you the freedom to change your own circumstance like this country. Whether it's taking a second job, changing your existing job, starting a business, whatever it might be – the power is in your hands! Never forget that. Champions are made when people make up their mind to make great things happen in their lives. If this book does nothing else – I hope it inspires you in some small way to become a champion.

God Bless. May you find the peace and happiness you are seeking.

NOTES:

NOTES:

FIXED COSTS WORKSHEET

The bills you know you always have to pay:

Mortgage	$_____
Rent	$_____
Student Loans	$_____
Car Loans	$_____
Power	$_____
Gas	$_____
Water	$_____
Phones	$_____
Television	$_____
Dry cleaning	$_____
Day care	$_____
Tithe	$_____
Neighborhood Dues	$_____
Other dues/memberships	$_____
Tuition	$_____
City	$_____
Insurance	$_____
Prescriptions	$_____
Other	$_____
Other	$_____
Other	$_____
Other	$_____
Other	$_____

TOTAL

DAILY SPEND WORKSHEET

Step 1: Identify how much money you take home per month.

(After all withdrawals) $_____

Step 2: Subtract out your fixed costs –
From *FIXED COSTS* worksheet.
TOTAL: $_____

Step 3: What's left over?
(Subtract Step 2 from Step 1): $_____

You now have a bucket of money left over. How much of that are you going to spend on essentials, i.e. Food and Gasoline?

Step 4: Essential Costs
Food per month $_____
Gasoline per month $_____
TOTAL: $_____

Step 5: What's left over now?
(Subtract Step 4 from Step 3): $_____

Step 6: How much are you going to save? $_____

Step 7: Determine your Daily Spend.
Subtract Step 6 from Step 5: $_____

Divide this amount by the number of days
         In your pay period: $_____

DAILY SPEND TOTAL = $_____

NOTES:

SAMPLE CALENDAR WORKSHEET

A = AVAILABLE: Money available per day (DAILY SPEND).

U = USED: How much you actually spent that day.

D = DIFFERENCE: Difference between DAILY SPEND and what USED.

$ __ / day

Sun	Mon	Tues	Wed	Thurs	Fri	Sat
A: U: D:	A: U: D:	A: U: D:	A: U: D:	A: U: D:	A: U: D:	A: U: D:
Sun	Mon	Tues	Wed	Thurs	Fri	Sat
A: U: D:	A: U: D:	A: U: D:	A: U: D:	A: U: D:	A: U: D:	A: U: D:
Sun	Mon	Tues	Wed	Thurs	Fri	Sat
A: U: D:	A: U: D:	A: U: D:	A: U: D:	A: U: D:	A: U: D:	A: U: D:
Sun	Mon	Tues	Wed	Thurs	Fri	Sat
A: U: D:	A: U: D:	A: U: D:	A: U: D:	A: U: D:	A: U: D:	A: U: D:
Sun	Mon	Tues	Wed	Thurs	Fri	Sat
A: U: D:	A: U: D:	A: U: D:	A: U: D:	A: U: D:	A: U: D:	A: U: D:

FOOD :	SPENT	DATE	TOTAL		GAS :	SPENT	DATE	TOTAL
$_____WEEK 1					$_____WEEK 1			
$_____WEEK 2					$_____WEEK 2			
$_____WEEK 3					$_____WEEK 3			
$_____WEEK 4					$_____WEEK 4			

NOTES:

NET WORTH WORKSHEET
Date (update quarterly): _____ / _____ / _____
Net Worth Goal: $_____

ASSETS (What you OWN)

Home Value	$_____
Retirement Account 1	$_____
Retirement Account 2	$_____
Stocks 1	$_____
Stocks 2	$_____
Education Account 1	$_____
Education Account 2	$_____
Savings 1	$_____
Savings 2	$_____
Checking	$_____
Medical	$_____
Vehicle 1	$_____
Vehicle 2	$_____
Vehicle 3	$_____
Other	$_____
Other	$_____
TOTAL ASSETS	$_____

LIABILITIES (What you OWE)

Home Mortgage	$_____
Unpaid Taxes	$_____
Car Debt 1	$_____
Car Debt 2	$_____
Credit Card Debt	$_____
Student Loans	$_____
Other	$_____
TOTAL LIABILITIES	$_____

NET WORTH (*OWN* minus *OWE*):

NOTES:

NOTES:

NOTES: